THE REAL ESTATE STRATEGY PLANNER

THE REAL ESTATE STRATEGY PLANNER

Craft Your Personal Real Estate Portfolio for Lasting Financial Freedom

Dave Meyer

BiggerPockets®
PUBLISHING
Denver, Colorado

VISIT

www.biggerpockets.com/strategybook

to download the accompanying
STRATEGY TOOL KIT
to plan your portfolio, track your deals, assess
your finances, and more!

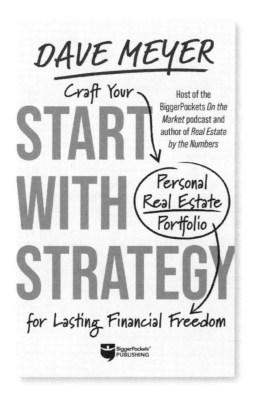

*Supercharge your portfolio planning
using the skills and lessons learned in*
Start with Strategy.

The Real Estate Strategy Planner: Craft Your Personal Real Estate Portfolio for Lasting Financial Freedom
Dave Meyer

Published by BiggerPockets Publishing LLC, Denver, CO
Copyright © 2023 by Dave Meyer
All rights reserved.

Publisher's Cataloging-in-Publication Data
Names: Meyer, Dave, 1987-, author.
Title: The real estate strategy planner : craft your personal real estate portfolio for lasting financial freedom / Dave Meyer.
Description: Denver, CO: BiggerPockets Publishing LLC, 2024.
Identifiers: ISBN: 9781960178244
Subjects: LCSH Real estate investment--United States. | Investments. | Finance, Personal. | BISAC BUSINESS & ECONOMICS / Real Estate / General | BUSINESS & ECONOMICS / Investments & Securities / Real Estate | BUSINESS & ECONOMICS / Personal Finance / Investing
Classification: LCC HD1382.5.M49 2024 | DDC 332.6324--dc23

Printed on recycled paper in Canada
MBP 10 9 8 7 6 5 4 3 2 1

TABLE OF CONTENTS

Part I
Foundations

Part II
Vision

Part III
Deal Design

Part IV
Portfolio Management

INTRODUCTION

Creating a personalized real estate investing strategy is a fun and empowering exercise. It a proven ticket to financial freedom, and you should be proud of yourself for taking the time to pursue it.

Start With Strategy contains all of the information, frameworks, and exercises you need to craft your unique strategy. But there's one thing I couldn't fit in the book—space for you to work through the many big, bold questions that arise when developing your strategy. What are your personal values? How much money do you want? What deal designs work best for you? On the surface these questions seem easy to answer, but that's not always the case!

Developing your own strategy is rarely a quick or linear process. Often you need time to think. A place to brainstorm. To iterate. You start with one idea, then change it up. Maybe a conversation with a friend alters your thinking. Sometimes you get stuck on a particular question and need to come back to it days later. There's nothing wrong with this—it's actually to be expected! Every time I revisit my own strategy, it takes several iterations and revisions to get it right.

This journal is the space for to work through every strategic decision required for building a successful portfolio. Use it to take notes. Write out ideas. Scribble in the margins. Cross things out. Let things get a little messy. This is a place for you to freely consider all of your options, and then organize your thoughts and ideas into a Personalized Real Estate Portfolio.

The journal is organized into four parts, just like the book. Part 1 of the book reviews the fundamentals that underpin your strategy, and in the journal, there is space for you to take notes about the opportunities and tradeoffs you need to consider. In Parts 2–4 the journal will be focused on helping you complete your Personalized Real Estate Portfolio (PREP). Part 2 will focus on your Vision and provides exercises and questions to help you think about where you want your portfolio to take you. Part 3 will give you space to dream up different Deal Designs that support your Vision. And in Part 4, you'll develop your Investment Thesis, Action Plan, and Buy Box.

After each Part, make sure to transfer your decisions into the PREP framework you'll find on pages 12–13. There will be places to write down your decisions along the way, but filling out a single PREP with all of your decisions visible in one play is the ultimate goal of this journal. There is great power in seeing your vision, deal design, and portfolio management plan all together in one place. It allows you double check your strategy to make sure everything is in alignment. You can also easily share it with other investors, and your community to get feedback. And at the very least, it will inspire you, motivate you and keep you on track toward your long-term goals.

The journal is designed to provide you with tools and exercises for a full year. Most people will only need to revisit their Vision and Deal Design annually, and so there is just one set of exercises and tools contained within. Portfolio Management, however, should be revisited four times per year (quarterly). As such, when you get to Part 4 you will find four of every exercise.

This is probably self-evident, but it's worth mentioning that this journal is not a standalone tool—it's a complement to *Start With Strategy*. A tool to further assist you in developing your own strategy. You won't get a lot out of this journal unless you read the book. If you get stuck or confused by any of these exercises, the best place to seek clarity is in the book. That said, how you use the journal is up to you. You can work through the journal concurrently as you read *Start with Strategy*, or you can read the entirety of *Start with Strategy*, then turn to the journal. Either works. And don't forget to use the other tool you get from this book—the Strategy Tool Kit. The spreadsheets and tools contained within further compliment the exercises and questions in this journal. (You can find the Tool Kit at www.biggerpockets.com/strategybook.)

As you work through this fun, challenging, and exciting process, remember one of the primary lessons of *Start With Strategy*: there is no *right* answer when it comes to real estate investing. Only *right for you*. So don't worry about what resources you have (or lack), what your risk tolerance is, or what other people think. This is about you, and your unique goals—whatever they might be. Being honest with yourself about what you want, and what you'll contribute to your portfolio gives you the best possible chance of success. Have fun, work hard, and enjoy the process of defining your strategy—it may just change your life.

MASTER PREP

Here is your Master PREP that you will fill out throughout the workbook. We reduce this down and provide instructions on how to fill out each of these individual parts. Return to this page as you complete your PREP work!

 ## VISION

Personal Values

Resource Audit

Money:

Time:

Current Skills:

Risk Profile

Time Horizon:

Risk Tolerance:

Risk Capacity:

Current Risk Profile:

Transactional Income Plan

Financial Goals

Reinvestment Rate:

Residual Income Goal:

Portfolio Value Goal:

DEAL DESIGN

Deal Type

Ownership Structure

Financing

Operational Plan

Management Plan

Asset Class

Location

Property Class

PORTFOLIO MANAGEMENT

Portfolio Performance

Total Equity:
Total Cash Flow:
Average ROE:
Average Risk:
Monthly Time Committed:

Market Conditions and Benchmarks

Scaling Plans

Resource Allocation

Investment Thesis

Action Plan

Buy Box

PART I
FOUNDATIONS

VISION

DEAL DESIGN

PORTFOLIO MANAGEMENT

hope you're excited to get to work on your personal strategy and start filling in the PREP template. That part is definitely the most fun and exciting, but don't race into it!

Before you start making big decisions about your portfolio, you need to understand the fundamentals that will drive the performance and composition of your portfolio. Think of it like reading the instruction manual before using a new appliance, device, or anything else. Taking some time upfront to learn the basics will save you time, and ensure you get the most out of your real estate strategy. Even if you're an experienced investor, I highly recommend you review the fundamentals before proceeding.

Part 1 of the book talks about resources, income types, compounding, profit drivers, risk, liquidity, and more. I packed a lot of information in. It's all relevant and important, but no one expects you to memorize everything in there. Instead, use the pages in the Journal to take notes on the key concepts you learn, and any ideas you may want to revisit later when you're filling in your PREP.

To me, the most important concept present throughout Part 1 is that real estate portfolios are full of tradeoffs. What resources do you want to use? Will you continue to earn transactional income, or retire as early as possible? Do you want to live off your residual income, or reinvest your profits? Everyone will weigh these tradeoffs differently, and I encourage you to write out your feelings and preferences for each of these tradeoffs in your notes. Coming back to these notes will be a big help later.

Time to dig in.

Use this space to take notes on **Chapter 1—The Resource Triangle**

Use this space to take notes on **Chapter 2—Understanding the Different Types of Income**

Use this space to take notes on **Chapter 3—Earning Your Return**

Use this space to take notes on **Chapter 4—Profit Drivers**

Use this space to take notes on **Chapter 5—Managing Risk**

Use this space to take notes on **Chapter 6—Funding Your Portfolio**

Use this space to take notes on **Chapter 7—Time Horizon**

Use this space to take notes on **Chapter 8—Liquidity**

PART II
VISION

VISION

DEAL DESIGN

PORTFOLIO MANAGEMENT

Now that you have a confident understanding of the fundamentals, it's time to get personal. From here on out, the focus of the journal will be to help you think through your personal strategic decisions. In Part 2, you'll define your vision.

Vision is the first step in personalizing your strategy because it gives you a clear target to aim for. Vision is the destination. There are five elements of Vision: personal values, transactional income plan, resource audit, risk assessment, and goal setting. As you'll likely notice, Vision is more about you and what you want, and less about actual real estate tactics. For some, vision comes easily since it's all about them. But for most people (and definitely for me), Vision is one of the tricker pieces of portfolio strategy, because it requires a lot of self-reflection.

The journal contains several exercises, and many questions for you to consider, to help you craft your vision. Think through these exercises carefully and remember—it's okay to take your time and to come back to the journal a few times before you finalize your Vision. Because Vision is so personal, it can be helpful to talk to friends, a significant other, family, and broader community about your Vision before writing anything on your PREP. You can also use some of the tools included in the Strategy Toolkit. But make sure not to draw out the process too long because you need a Vision to move on to other parts of your PREP, and to start executing on your strategy! Once you feel confident in your Vision, write it on Page 53, and on your master PREP file on Pages 12-13.

As you progress in your investing career, you'll likely want to check in on your Vision once per year, and make sure everything still holds up. I find that Vision changes less for me than the other pieces of my PREP, but that's just me. If your Vision changes in the future, just make that change in your annual PREP update.

But enough about future iterations—go define your Vision!

PERSONAL VALUES

STRATEGIC DECISION: To complete the Personal Values section of your PREP, create a list of your Personal Values. You should have no more than five personal values, and they should be written simply.

In the literal sense, your Personal Values are simple things: just a few words on your PREP Yet, for most people, narrowing down what they actually value most in life is a challenging—but very rewarding—process Your Personal Values are the things you care about most in life, and getting really clear about your values takes self-reflection.

The objective of the following exercises is for you to write down no more than five Personal Values, each of which is only a few words Each Personal Value should represent something you care about deeply It should be something you cannot live without. Since I'm sure you care about many things, it can be tempting to write down a lot of values, but that defeats the purpose The benefit of your Personal Values is to narrow focus and provide clarity Having too many values will create complexity, not clarity Strive for as few and as simple Personal Values as possible.

If you happen to be someone who can very easily write down your Personal Values, go ahead and write them down. For full instructions, see pages 135–139 in *Start with Strategy*.

STEP 1: THE INITIAL LIST

The first step in setting your Personal Values is to consider a broad number of options, and to choose those that resonate with you.

1. Review the list of potential core values below
2. Circle all worlds that resonate with you. Aim to have 10–20.
3. If there are values you want to add that aren't on the list, that's great! Write them in the blank space on the next page.

CORE VALUES

Abundance	Contribution	Freedom	Meaning	Simplicity
Acceptance	Control	Friendship	Moderation	Sincerity
Accomplishment	Cooperation	Fun	Motivation	Skillfulness
Accountability	Courage	Generosity	Obedience	Solitude
Accuracy	Courtesy	Giving	Openness	Speed
Achievement	Creativity	Goodness	Optimism	Spirituality
Adaptability	Credibility	Grace	Order	Stability
Adventure	Curiosity	Gratitude	Organization	Status
Affection	Decisiveness	Growth	Originality	Stewardship
Alertness	Dedication	Happiness	Passion	Strength
Ambition	Dependability	Hard Work	Patience	Structure
Assertiveness	Determination	Harmony	Patriotism	Success
Attentive	Devotion	Health	Peace	Support
Authenticity	Dignity	Honesty	Playfulness	Surprise
Awareness	Discipline	Honor	Poise	Sustainability
Balance	Diversity	Humility	Positivity	Teamwork
Beauty	Efficiency	Humor	Power	Temperance
Boldness	Empathy	Imagination	Productivity	Thankful
Bravery	Endurance	Independence	Professionalism	Thorough
Brilliance	Energy	Individuality	Prosperity	Thoughtful
Calmness	Enjoyment	Inner Harmony	Purpose	Timeliness
Capable	Enthusiasm	Innovation	Quality	Tolerance
Careful	Equality	Insightful	Recognition	Toughness
Caring	Ethical	Inspiring	Respect	Traditional
Certainty	Excellence	Integrity	Responsibility	Tranquility
Challenge	Excitement	Intelligence	Restraint	Transparency
Charity	Experience	Intuitive	Results-oriented	Trustworthy
Cleanliness	Expertise	Joy	Rigor	Understanding
Clear	Exploration	Justice	Security	Uniqueness
Clever	Fairness	Kindness	Self-actualization	Unity
Comfort	Faith	Knowledge	Self-development	Vision
Commitment	Fame	Lawful	Self-reliance	Vitality
Communication	Family	Leadership	Self-respect	Wealth
Community	Fearless	Learning	Selfless	Welcoming
Compassion	Fidelity	Logic	Sensitivity	Winning
Competence	Fitness	Love	Serenity	Wisdom
Confidence	Focus	Loyalty	Service	
Consistency	Foresight	Mastery	Sharing	
Contentment	Forgiveness	Maturity	Silence	

Other values not on list:

_____

_____

_____

_____

STEP 2: PRUNE IT DOWN

Get your list of words down to 5 or fewer. Carefully consider what you highlighted above, and then narrow down your list to five or fewer values. The remaining words should represent the things you value most in life, and cannot live without.

_____

_____

_____

_____

_____

STEP 3: MAKE IT YOUR OWN

Tweak the words you've selected so they feel motivating, and personalized to you. This will be your final list of personal values. Once you have a finalized list of personalized values, write them down in your PREP.

_____

_____

_____

_____

_____

COMMENTS/NOTES:

TRANSACTIONAL INCOME PLAN

The point of your TIP is just to write out a sentence or two about how you plan to earn your transactional income going forward It can be as simple as "Stay at my current job indefinitely" or could entail a complete career change. Work through the following questions to develop your own Transactional Income Plan.

Transactional income sources (AKA, your job) can provide your with resources, and fulfillment. But not all jobs offer differing amounts.

If you haven't already done so, take a moment right now and figure out which quadrant your current jobs fall into. How fulfilling is your current job? Is it providing you with resources you can contribute to your portfolio? If you're not currently employed, think about prior jobs or jobs you're interested in.

This exercise should help you decide if you want to keep working in your current job, or find something else.

QUADRANT NUMBER *(Circle)*

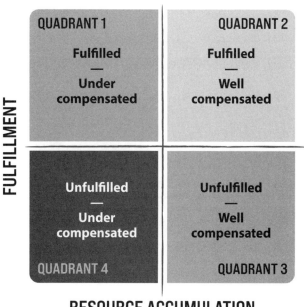

LET'S WRITE YOUR TRANSACTIONAL INCOME PLAN.

Do you plan to keep earning transactional income?

Are you satisfied with your current source of transactional income (AKA job)?

Are you interested in going into real estate full-time?

What other transactional income sources appeal to you?

How could acquire more resources?

Are there ways you could feel more fulfilled (and do you care about that)?

_____

_____

_____

_____

_____

_____

_____

_____

ADDITIONAL QUESTIONS TO ASK YOURSELF.

What do my values tell me about how I could and should be earning transactional income?

_____

_____

_____

Do I find my current work meaningful beyond the resources it provides me?

_____

_____

Does my current means of earning transactional income provide me with resources that will help me build a real estate portfolio?

_____

_____

Is my current source of transactional income stable and secure? Is that a priority (maybe even a higher priority than a real estate portfolio) to me and my family?

_____

_____

How difficult would it be for me to find a transactional income source that paid better? Or offered me more fulfillment?

_____

_____

_____

Would transactional income from the real estate industry put me in a better position to build my portfolio?

_____

_____

Would a real estate job like flipping, wholesaling, or real estate services offer the same benefits (healthcare, paid time off, etc.) as my current job?

_____

_____

Would it make it easier or harder to get a loan? Find partners?

_____

_____

Do I want my entire career to be dependent on one industry, which can be cyclical? Or do I want to hedge my income streams by working across industries?

_____

_____

Can I augment my resources through gig work, part-time work, or volunteering, above and beyond my current job?

_____

_____

Please write out your TIP.

Once you've made your TIP decision, add it to your PREP!

RESOURCE AUDIT: TIME, SKILL, AND CAPITAL

Every portfolio needs the same three resources: time, capital, and skill. In the Resource Audit, you need to decide what resources you'll contribute to your portfolio. Below are instructions, exercises, and questions to walk you through your decisions about each of the three resources. For full instructions, see pages 152–154 in *Start with Strategy*.

 Use the Excel Toolkit located on www.BiggerPockets.com/strategybook throughout this section.

TIME AUDIT

STRATEGIC DECISION: To complete the Time piece of your PREP's Resource Audit, set an intention for how much time you will commit to your real estate portfolio on a monthly basis. In the Time Audit, you will determine how much time you are going to personally commit to building your real estate portfolio. For some people, this may be really easy. For those who are tight on time, I recommend start by creating a Time Budget. A Time Budget is a simple exercise where you visualize how you're spending your time, and identify areas where you may be able to reallocate time towards your portfolio.

TIME BUDGET EXERCISE

1. Write out every activity you do regularly. This can be anything! Work, sleep, family commitments, hobbies, or anything else. If you do it regularly, and it takes up time, write it down.
2. Write how many hours you average on each activity per week.
3. Assess how big of a priority each activity is by ranking them as either non-negotiable (unwilling to change your time commitment), high (very little flexibility on time spent), medium (some flexibility, and low (very flexible).

Here is an example of a completed Time Budget Exercise.

ACTIVITY	TIME COMMITMENT (HOURS)	PRIORITY
Personal/Family Time	20	Non Negotiable
Sleep	52.5	Non Negotiable
Mental & Physical Health	10	Non Negotiable
Work at BiggerPockets	50	High
Social Life	10	High
Book/Data Deli/Etc.	10	Medium
House Work/Errands	7	Medium
Unstructured Free Time	7	Low
Total	**166.5**	
Hours Per Week	**168**	
Time for Real Estate	**1.5**	

Fill out your Time Budget Exercise below.

ACTIVITY	TIME COMMITMENT (HOURS)	PRIORITY
Total		
Hours Per Week		
Time for Real Estate		

Interpreting your results

Once you've accounted for how your time is being spent currently, consider your results. If you have extra time leftover, that's great! You can allocate that towards your portfolio. If you don't have enough time, think through what activities you'd be willing to shift hours away from, in order to build your portfolio. Remember, all portfolios require time—especially when you're starting out!

Make sure to take some time to consider your time commitment carefully. Discuss it with friends and family and decide what you're willing to commit. When you're ready, write your time commitment down below, and on your PREP.

Total Time Commitment _____

SKILL AUDIT

STRATEGIC DECISION: To complete the Skill part of your PREP's Resource Audit, determine what skills you'll be dedicating to your portfolio yourself and which you will source externally. On your PREP, only write the skills you will commit. For full instructions, see pages 161–164 in *Start with Strategy*.

SKILL BUDGET EXERCISE

Determining what skills you'll bring to your portfolio is an often overlooked element of portfolio strategy—but its super important! No one can build a portfolio alone, and you should take the time to decide what skills you can, and want, to contribute, and what you'll outsource.

1. For each skill give an honest assessment of how competent you are at the skill as high, medium or low.
2. If you're less than 'high' in any skill, make a subjective assessment of how hard it will be for you to improve at that skill.
3. Decide which skills are worthwhile for you to contribute, which you are better off acquiring, and which you'll use a hybrid model for.

Here is an example of a completed Skill Audit.

SKILL	CURRENT SKILL LEVEL	DIFFICULTY TO LEARN	CONTRIBUTE/ ACQUIRE
Portfolio Strategy	High		Contribute
Deal Flow	Medium	Medium	Hybrid
Deal Analysis	High		Contribute
Operations	Medium	Medium	Contribute
Networking	Medium	Medium	Contribute
Securing Financing	Medium	Low	Contribute
Finance & Tax	Low	High	Acquire
Market Analysis	High	Medium	Contribute
Tenant Management	Medium	High	Hybrid
Repairs & Maintenance	Low	High	Acquire
Construction & Capital Improvements	Low	High	Acquire
Transacting	Low	High	Acquire

Fill out your Skill Audit below.

SKILL	CURRENT SKILL LEVEL	DIFFICULTY TO LEARN	CONTRIBUTE/ACQUIRE
Portfolio Strategy			
Deal Flow			
Deal Analysis			
Operations			
Networking			
Securing Financing			
Finance & Tax			
Market Analysis			
Tenant Management			
Repairs & Maintenance			
Construction & Capital Improvements			
Transacting			

Once you've decided what skills you're going to contribute and acquire, write your time commitment down below, and on your PREP. Remember this can and will change over time, but you need to set an intention for at least the coming year.

CAPITAL AUDIT

STRATEGIC DECISION: To complete the Capital part of your PREP's Resource Audit, calculate your discretionary income, net worth, and investable assets. These are all essential numbers you'll need to grow your portfolio. For full instructions, see pages 169–171 in *Start with Strategy*.

DISCRETIONARY INCOME

WHAT IT IS: The monthly income you have left over after covering expenses
HOW TO CALCULATE IT: Total Income – Total Expenses
1. In the fields below add up all of your monthly income, and monthly expenses, similar to the example below.
2. Add up all your Income, and write it in the Total Income box. Then, add up all your expenses in the Total Expenses box.
3. Subtract your total expenses from your total income to get your discretionary income.

Here is an example of a completed Capital Audit.

DISCRETIONARY INCOME: CHLOE FRANKLIN
As of December 31, 2023

Income	Estimated Value	Expenses	Estimated Value
Salary	$4,500	Mortgage	$1,623.00
Freelancing	$600	Car payment	$325.00
		Student Loan Payment	$280.00
		Food & Groceries	$400.00
		Entertainment	$350.00
		Gym	$60.00
		Gas	$100.00
		Misc	$500.00
Total Income	**$5,100.00**	**Total Expenses**	**$3,638.00**
Discretionary Income			**$1,462.00**

Fill out your Capital Audit below.

DISCRETIONARY INCOME:

As of _____

Income	Estimated Value	Expenses	Estimated Value
Total Income		**Total Expenses**	
Discretionary Income			

Once you've calculated your discretionary income, write it in your PREP.

NET WORTH

WHAT IT IS: The total value of everything you own (assets) minus everything you owe (liabilities)

HOW TO CALCULATE IT: Total Assets − Total Liabilities

1. In the fields below add up all of your assets in the Assets Column. Then add all of your Liabilities in the Liabilities column.
2. Add up all your Assets and write it in the Total Assets box. Then, add up all your liabilities in the Total Liabilities box.
3. Subtract your total assets from your total liabilities to get your discretionary income.

Remember this doesn't need to be super precise. You want to be accurate, but rounding is ok.

Here is an example of how to evaluate your Net Worth.

PERSONAL FINANCIAL STATEMENT: CHLOE FRANKLIN
As of December 31, 2023

Assets	Estimated Value	Liabilities	Estimated Value
Cash or Cash Equivalent		**Loans**	
Cash on Hand	$500.00	Mortgage - Personal Residence	$248,000.00
Bank - Checking Account	$2,500.00	School Loan	$55,000.00
Bank - Savings Account	$18,000.00	Car Loan	$14,600.00
Retirement Accounts		**Revolving Debt**	
Self-Directed IRA	$22,000.00	Credit Cards	$1,200.00
Investments		**Other**	
Stocks	$24,000.00		
Bonds	$6,000.00		
Real/Personal Property Owned			
Personal Residence	$345,000.00		
2018 Nissan Altima	$18,000.00		
Jewelry	$2,000.00		
Assets Total	**$438,000.00**	**Liabilities Total**	**$318,800.00**
Estimated Net Worth:			**$119,200.00**

Fill out your Net Worth assessment below.

PERSONAL FINANCIAL STATEMENT

As of _____

Assets	Liabilities
Estimated Value	Estimated Value
Cash or Cash Equivalent	**Loans**
Retirement Accounts	**Revolving Debt**
Investments	**Other**
Real/Personal Property Owned	
Assets Total	**Liabilities Total**
Estimated Net Worth:	

Once you've calculated your Net Worth, write it in your PREP.

INVESTABLE ASSETS

WHAT IT IS: The capital you have today to invest in real estate

HOW TO CALCULATE IT: Liquid Assets – Emergency Reserves

1. Decide assets you can, and want to invest in real estate. Write them down in the fields below, along with the total amount.
2. Sum all of your investible assets, and cash into the 'Committed Assets' box.
3. Determine how many months of cash reserves you want (as least 3!), and multiply it by your total monthly expenses (which you calculated above). Write the result down under total reserves.
4. Subtract your total reserves from your committed assets to calculate your investible assets. Write that down.

Here is an example of how to determine your Investable Assets.

INVESTABLE ASSETS: CHLOE FRANKLIN
As of December 31, 2023

Assets	
	Estimated Value
Cash or Cash Equivalent	
Cash on Hand	$500.00
Bank - Checking Account	$2,500.00
Bank - Savings Account	$18,000.00
Investments	
Stocks	$24,000.00
Bonds	$6,000.00
Committed Assets	**$51,000.00**
Total Reserve	$10,914.00
Investable Assets	**$40,086.00**

Fill out your Investable Assets below.

INVESTABLE ASSETS:

As of _____

Assets	
	Estimated Value
Cash or Cash Equivalent	
Investments	
Committed Assets	
Total Reserve	
Investable Assets	

Once you've calculated your Investible Assets, write it in your PREP.

PUTTING IT ALL TOGETHER

Consolidate your financial audit results below, and write out any notes or thoughts you have about this exercise.

Discretionary Income _____

Net worth _____

Investable Assets _____

COMMENTS/NOTES:

RISK ASSESSMENT

STRATEGIC DECISION: Define your time horizon, risk tolerance, and risk capacity. Then consolidate them into a guiding policy on how you'll use risk in your portfolio. Once you've done that, write them in the Risk Profile section of your PREP. For full instructions, see pages 181–183 in *Start with Strategy*.

TIME HORIZON

Your time horizon is the point at which you want to be able to live off your portfolio's residual income.

Questions to ask yourself about your time horizon.

Is retiring your primary objective for real estate investing? Or are you willing to work longer to reduce risk and improve growth potential?

How ambitious are your financial goals? The more ambitious you are, the longer your time horizon will need to be.

Do you want to stop working altogether or are you more interested in being "work-optional"?

Are you comfortable with a relatively common retirement age of 65 or would you prefer to move it earlier? Or do you love your work and plan to work beyond a traditional retirement age?

My Time Horizon (in years): _____

*When you have an idea of what you want your Time Horizon to be,
write it down in your PREP.*

RISK TOLERANCE

Your Risk Tolerance is a subjective measurement of how comfortable you are with taking risks. Consider the following questions, and write down any feelings you have about risk before writing down your risk tolerance.

Questions to ask yourself about your Risk Tolerance.

How do you feel about risk in non-investment parts of your life? Are you a thrill seeker or do you prefer to play it safe most of the time?

_____

_____

What is more important to you: protecting the money you have or maximizing your returns? The more you look to maximize your returns, the more risk you will need to take.

_____

_____

Are you willing to accept principal loss in order to maximize returns?

_____

_____

If you saw your portfolio value decline by 10 percent or more, what would you do? Would you sell to avoid further losses or would you ride it out?

_____

_____

How would you feel if the housing market experienced high volatility for a year or two? Are you comfortable riding out volatility in the service of long-term benefit?

_____

_____

My Risk Tolerance (circle):

1	3	5
(Conservative)	(Moderate)	(Aggressive)

←――――――――――――――――――――――――――――――――――→

RISK CAPACITY

The last part of the risk assessment is how able you are to take risk—regardless of your comfort with it. Below are questions to help you determine your own Risk Capacity. Write down your thoughts.

Questions to ask yourself about your Risk Capacity.

How experienced are you in real estate investing? The more experienced you are, the higher your risk capacity. If you've never done a deal, or are on your first one, you will likely have a low risk capacity.

_____

_____

What is your transactional income and personal cash flow situation? How stable is that income? The more cash you generate from outside your portfolio, and the more stable that income, the higher your risk capacity.

_____

_____

How much principal do you plan to add to your portfolio? The more principal you plan to add over the course of your time horizon, the higher your capacity for risk.

_____

_____

_____

What is your family situation? Do others depend on you for financial stability and support? If you need a good deal of liquidity to support your lifestyle, your capacity for risk will be low.

_____

_____

_____

My Risk Capacity (Circle):

1	3	5
(Conservative)	**(Moderate)**	**(Aggressive)**

←—————————————————————→

PUTTING IT ALL TOGETHER

The last part of the risk assessment is how able you are to take risk—regardless of your comfort with it. Below are questions to help you determine your own Risk Capacity. Write down your thoughts.

_____

_____

_____

_____

_____

_____

_____

_____

_____

_____

_____

_____

My Risk Profile:

The last step is to create a single score for your Risk Profile from 1 to 5, with 1 being the most conservative, and 5 being the most aggressive. Consider your time horizon, risk tolerance, and risk capacity, and then set the risk profile you will pursue with your portfolio

Time Horizon

_____

Risk Tolerance

_____

Risk Capacity

_____

Risk Profile

_____

FINANCIAL GOALS

> **STRATEGIC DECISION:** To complete the Financial Goals section of your PREP, create a cash flow goal and a portfolio value goal. Think hard about what you actually want and need before setting these goals. Once you have them, write them in your PREP. For full instructions, see pages 189–194 in *Start with Strategy*.

CASHFLOW GOAL

Step 1: Reimagine Current Expenses

- Start with a baseline of where you are today!
- Revisit your Resource Audit and find your listed expenses.
    - Go line by line and determine how each expenses will change over time.
- Consider your Time Horizon as you estimate future expenses.

Step 2: What's New?

- Add any new expenses you're anticipating

Step 3: Reinvestment

Step 4: Account for Inflation

- Remember, the general rule of thumb that spending power halves every 30 years.

Step 5: Make it SMART

- Specific
- Measurable
- Achievable
- Relevant
- Time-Bound

Here is an example of how to determine your Financial Goals.

CASH FLOW GOAL: CHLOE FRANKLIN
As of December 31, 2023

Time Horizon (Years)	15

Income		Expenses	
	Estimated Value		Estimated Value
Transactional Income		**Expenses**	
Salary	$0	Mortgage	$2,800
Freelancing	$0	Second Home Mortgage	$2,000
		Car Payment	$600
		Student Loan Payment	$-
		Food & Groceries	$800
Transactional Income Total	$0	Entertainment	$750
		Gym	$90
		Gas	$100
		Medical Insurance	$500
		Misc.	$1,000
		Portfolio Reinvestment	$1,000
Monthly Cash Flow Goal	**$14,460**	**Total Expenses (current dollars)**	**$9,640**
Annual Cash Flow Goal	**$173,520**	**Annual Expenses (current dollars)**	**$115,680.00**
Total Monthly Income at Time Horizon	**$14,460**	**Estimated Expenses at Time Horizon**	**$14,460**

Personal Cash Flow	
Monthly Cash Flow Goal	$14,460
Annual Cash Flow Goal	$173,520
Expected Return on Equity	5%
Minimum Portfolio Value Goal	$3,470,400

Fill out your Financial Goals below.

CASH FLOW GOAL:

As of _____

Time Horizon (Years) _____

Income		Expenses	
	Estimated Value		Estimated Value
Transactional Income		**Expenses**	
Transactional Income Total $			

Monthly Cash Flow Goal		**Total Expenses (current dollars)**	
Annual Cash Flow Goal		**Annual Expenses (current dollars)**	
Total Monthly Income at Time Horizon		**Estimated Expenses at Time Horizon**	
Personal Cash Flow			

Monthly Cash Flow Goal _____

Annual Cash Flow Goal _____

SMART Cashflow Goal _____

PORTFOLIO VALUE GOAL

This is the number you get when you add up the equity in all of your real estate investments. You can easily calculate this using your Portfolio Goal from above, and an estimate Return on Equity for your entire portfolio.

Annual Cashflow Goal: _____

Estimate Return on Equity (ROE): _____

Simply divide your cashflow goal, by your estimated ROE, and get your minimum portfolio value. Remember, you can always add some padding if you want!

Cashflow _____ *÷ Estimated ROE =* *Minimum Portfolio Value* _____ *+ Padding:*

SMART Portfolio Value Goal _____

COMMENTS/NOTES: _____

VISION STATEMENT

Let's put it all together now. Complete the following based on your work in Part I.

VALUES

_____
_____
_____
_____
_____

RESOURCES

Time Commitment: _____

Skills Commitment: _____

Discretionary Income: _____

Net Worth: _____

Investable Assets: _____

RISK PROFILE

_____
_____
_____
_____

FINANCIAL GOALS

Cashflow Goal: _____

Portfolio Value Goal: _____

VISION

Personal Values

Resource Audit
Money:
Time:
Current Skills:

Risk Profile
Time Horizon:
Risk Tolerance:
Risk Capacity:
Current Risk Profile:

Transactional Income Plan

Financial Goals
Reinvestment Rate:

Residual Income Goal:

Portfolio Value Goal:

NOTES:

Use this space to take notes on your Vision Statement.

PART III
DEAL DESIGN

VISION

DEAL DESIGN

PORTFOLIO MANAGEMENT

In Part 3, you'll take the Vision you've crafted, and start to layer in real estate investing tactics that are appropriately aligned. You do that with Deal Design.

Deal Design is a framework comprised of eight unique elements that combine to make a deal. The eight elements are: deal type, financing, ownership structure, operating plan, management plan, asset class, market, and property class. The goal of Deal Design is to identify which tactics could help you achieve your vision. This is a 'select all that apply' type of exercise.

The next several chapters of the journal all follow the same pattern. First, you'll find space to take notes about the various options within each deal design element. Use this space to write down important lessons, and any follow up questions you have about each tactic. Next, you'll find questions to help guide your thinking. At the end of each chapter is a rubric. The rubric is an opportunity for you to score how well each option fits with your current resource levels and your risk and reward preferences. It also gives you space to determine which options will go on your PREP.

At the end of Part 3, make sure to write down all of the options you want to consider for future deals on Page 97, and in your master PREP on pages 12-13. In terms of frequency, you should only have to revisit your deal design annually. Remember, Deal Design isn't about picking your next deal right now. You're just identifying what deals you *could* do, based on your goals. So focus on giving yourself enough options to ensure you have strategic flexibility in the coming years, but not so many options that it becomes overwhelming.

What deal designs are right for you? Decide in the chapters that follow.

DEAL TYPES

STRATEGIC DECISION: Of the deal types explained in this chapter, which ones are aligned with your Vision and fit within your broader Portfolio Strategy? You don't need to make decisions now for your entire investing career—just select the deal types that fit your Vision for the next three years. Any deal types that fit your criteria should be written in your PREP. For full instructions, see pages 216–218 in *Start with Strategy*.

Questions to consider when determining Deal Types.

What deal types work with the current resources that you have?

How complex a business do you want to run?

Given your risk profile, what deal types make the most sense?

How do your values align with different deal types?

Do you have the specific skills needed for the deal types you want to use? How easy would it be for you to acquire or source those skills externally?

Do you need to prioritize residual income or transactional income?

How important are tax benefits to you?

What is the best way to learn so you can succeed in the long run?

Rental Properties

NOTES:

Short Term Rentals

NOTES:

Fix-and-Flip

NOTES:

Commercial

NOTES:

Development

NOTES:

Lending

NOTES:

Use this rubric to determine which Deal Types are aligned with your resources, and your risk/reward preferences. Then, decide which Deal Types belong on your PREP.

	Resource Alignment			Risk/Reward Alignment	
	Time	Capital	Skill		Include in PREP?
Rental Properties					
Short-Term Rentals					
Fix-and-Flip					
Commercial					
Development					
Lending					

OWNERSHIP STRUCTURE

STRATEGIC DECISION: Of the ownership structures explained in this chapter, which ones are aligned with your Vision and fit within your broader Portfolio Strategy? Your ownership structure can change for each deal you do, so make sure to consider any ownership structure that may work for you in the coming years. Any ownership structures that fit your criteria should be written in your PREP. For full instructions, see pages 225–226 in *Start with Strategy*.

Questions to ask yourself when determining your Ownership Structure.

Do you have sufficient capital to contribute to a deal? Or do you need to contribute time or skill to get started?

Are you willing to assume all the risk from a deal?

Would the performance of your deals benefit from the experience of a partner?

Do you work well with others or work better alone?

Are you an accredited investor?

Do you have a high-quality professional network where you can find good partners?

_____

_____

Are you comfortable giving up almost all control to a GP?

_____

_____

Can you responsibly raise money from others, and will you be a good steward of their capital?

_____

_____

Sole Ownership

NOTES:

Partnerships

NOTES:

Syndication/funds

Use this rubric to determine which Ownership Structures are aligned with your resources, and your risk/reward preferences. Then, decide which Ownership Structures belong on your PREP.

	Resource Alignment			Risk/Reward Alignment	Include in PREP?
	Time	Capital	Skill		
Sole Ownership					
Active Partnerships					
Passive Partnerships					
Time/Skill Partnerships					
Syndication					
Funds					

FINANCING

STRATEGIC DECISION: Of the financing options explained in this chapter, which ones are aligned with your Vision and fit within your broader Portfolio Strategy? Select any financing options that could work well for you and try to be as specific as possible. Will you use term loans, lines of credit, or both? What amortization schedules, LTVs, and interest rate structure will you pursue? Any financing options that fit your criteria should be written in your PREP. For full instructions, see pages 242–243 in *Start with Strategy*.

Select the financing options that align with your resources and broader portfolio strategy. Then write down any notes about financial types you may want to use.

Using Debt?

☐ YES ☐ NO

LOAN TO VALUE: *(Circle)*   High (>80%)   Standard (70–80%)   Low (<70%)

FIXED VS. ADJUSTABLE RATE: *(Circle)*   Fixed   Adjustable

AMORTIZATION SCHEDULE: *(Circle)*

Fully Amortized   Partially Amortized   Interest-only

Conventional

NOTES:

FHA

NOTES:

VA

NOTES:

Portfolio

NOTES:

Hard Money

NOTES:

Private Loans

NOTES:

Seller Financing

NOTES:

Subject-To

NOTES:

Debt Service Coverage Ration (DSCR)

NOTES:

Commercial Loans

NOTES:

LINES OF CREDIT

Home Equity Line of Credit (HELOC)

NOTES:

Business Line of Credit

NOTES:

Personal Line of Credit

NOTES:

Use this rubric to determine which Financing Options are aligned with your resources, and your risk/reward preferences. Then, decide which types of Financing belong on your PREP.

	Resource Alignment			Risk/Reward Alignment	Include in PREP?
	Time	Capital	Skill		
Equity (All Cash)					
Conventional Loan					
FHA Loan					
VA Loan					
Portfolio Loan					
Hard Money Loan					
Private Loan					
Seller Financing					
Subject-To					
DSCR Loan					
Commercial Loan					
Line of Credit					

You can use the BiggerPockets Lender Finder tool with Pro Membership to contact a lender. Use the information above when speaking with a lender.

OPERATING PLANS

STRATEGIC DECISION: Determine which operating plans are aligned with your Vision and fit within your broader Portfolio Strategy. Remember that operating plans can be combined together and are not mutually exclusive. Any operating plans that fit your criteria should be written in your PREP. For full instructions, see pages 252–253 in *Start with Strategy*.

Questions to consider when determining your Operating Plan.

How experienced are you as an investor? Certain operating plans favor newer investors (like owner occupancy), while others are better for experienced investors.

_____

_____

_____

What skills do you have? Operating plans are one of the most skill-dependent considerations in your Deal Design, and you should select plans that you can confidently execute on.

_____

_____

_____

_____

Are you willing to owner occupy? If so, it's a great way to get started (and is not nearly as awkward as many believe it to be).

_____

_____

_____

How can you combine multiple operating plans to achieve the maximum value of your deals?

_____

_____

_____

_____

_____

_____

_____

_____

Which operating plans will work well together across your portfolio to achieve the right balance of risk, reward, and liquidity?

_____

_____

_____

_____

_____

_____

Buy and Hold

NOTES:

Value-Add

NOTES:

BRRRR

NOTES:

Operational Efficiency

NOTES:

Owner Occupancy

NOTES:

Rent by the Room

NOTES:

Creative Opportunities

NOTES:

Use this rubric to determine which Operating Plans are aligned with your resources, and your risk/reward preferences. Then, decide which Operating Plans belong on your PREP.

	Resource Alignment			Risk/Reward Alignment	Include in PREP?
	Time	Capital	Skill		
Buy and Hold					
Value-Add					
BRRRR					
Operational Efficiency					
Rent by the Room					
Opportunistic					
Other:					

MANAGEMENT PLANS

STRATEGIC DECISION: Which management plans best support your Vision? Determine which management plans work with your current resources and write them in your PREP. For full instructions, see pages 258–259 in *Start with Strategy*.

Questions to consider when determining your Management Plan.

How much experience do you have? Active management is a great way to learn the business?

_____

_____

_____

How much time are you committing to your portfolio? Are you working full-time?

_____

_____

_____

Do you have any real estate skills that you can efficiently contribute to managing your portfolio?

_____

_____

_____

What skills are you better off buying or trading for than contributing yourself?

_____

_____

_____

Do you want to invest passively? Are you willing to pay third parties for both operational and asset management?

_____

_____

_____

Do you qualify as an accredited investor, and can you get access to truly passive deals?

_____

_____

_____

Active Management

┌─ *NOTES:* ─────────────────────────────────────┐
│   │
│   │
│   │
│   │
│   │
│   │
│   │
└───┘

Hybrid Management

┌─ *NOTES:* ─────────────────────────────────────┐
│   │
│   │
│   │
│   │
│   │
│   │
│   │
└───┘

Passive Management

Use this rubric to determine which Management Plans are aligned with your resources, and your risk/reward preferences. Then, decide which Management Plans belong on your PREP.

	Resource Alignment			Risk/Reward Alignment	
	Time	Capital	Skill		Include in PREP?
Active Management					
Hybrid Management					
Passive Management					

ASSET CLASSES

STRATEGIC DECISION: Which asset classes are best aligned with your Vision and fit within your broader strategy? The most important decision is whether you'll focus only on residential assets or on commercial assets or will be open to a combination of the two. When you've decided which asset classes are aligned with your strategy, write them in your PREP. For full instructions, see pages 271–272 in *Start with Strategy*.

RESIDENTIAL ASSETS

Questions to consider when determining Asset Classes.

How much capital do you have to invest? The capital requirements differ greatly between asset classes.

What are you prioritizing at this point in your investing career? Rapid scaling? Risk mitigation? Solid, predictable returns?

Are you willing to buy a property with an HOA or other governing body?

How sophisticated is your management plan? The bigger the asset, the more complex the operations. Make sure you're prepared.

Can you qualify for residential financing? If you can, it can help reduce risk and lower costs.

_____

_____

Do you want to focus on providing shelter, or are you interested in working with retail and office tenants?

_____

_____

Do you want to consider an owner-occupied deal type like house hacking or a live-in flip? These options are only possible for residential assets.

_____

_____

How can you invest in different asset classes to create diversification in your portfolio?

_____

_____

_____

_____

_____

Detached Single-Family Residence

NOTES:

Attached Single-Family Residence (Townhome/Co-op/Condo/Etc.)

┌─ *NOTES:* ──┐
│   │
│   │
│   │
│   │
│   │
│   │
└──┘

Small Multifamily

┌─ *NOTES:* ──┐
│   │
│   │
│   │
│   │
│   │
│   │
└──┘

COMMERCIAL ASSETS

Large Multifamily

┌─ *NOTES:* ──┐
│   │
│   │
│   │
│   │
│   │
│   │
└──┘

Mobile Home Parks

NOTES:

Self-Storage

NOTES:

Retail/Office/Industrial

NOTES:

Other

NOTES:

Use this rubric to determine which Asset Classes are aligned with your resources, and your risk/reward preferences. Then, decide which Asset Classes belong on your PREP.

	Resource Alignment			Risk/Reward Alignment	Include in PREP?
	Time	Capital	Skill		
Residential					
Detached SFR					
Attached SFR					
Small Multifamily					
Commercial					
Large Multifamily					
Self-Storage					
Mobile Homes					
Office/Retail/Industrial					

PICKING A MARKET

STRATEGIC DECISION: Select at least one market to include on your PREP. This could be your local market or somewhere "long-distance" (for help with that decision, see below). If you're new to investing, try to choose up to five markets to focus on. If you're experienced, you can select as many markets as is practical. Once you have chosen your target markets, write them in your PREP. For full instructions, see pages 284–287 in *Start with Strategy*.

Will you invest locally, long distance, or are you open to either?

LOCAL VS. LONG DISTANCE INVESTING *(Circle one)*   Local   Long Distance   Either

Select up to 5 markets to consider, and conduct market research by finding key data point. Sources for data are included in the book!

Market Research

Market 1

	CURRENT VALUE	YEAR OVER YEAR CHANGE	MONTHLY OVER MONTH CHANGE
Median Home Price			
Rent Price			
Rent-to-Price Ratio			
Wage Growth			
Unemployment Rate			

Market 2

	CURRENT VALUE	YEAR OVER YEAR CHANGE	MONTHLY OVER MONTH CHANGE
Median Home Price			
Rent Price			
Rent-to-Price Ratio			
Wage Growth			
Unemployment Rate			

Market 3

	CURRENT VALUE	YEAR OVER YEAR CHANGE	MONTHLY OVER MONTH CHANGE
Median Home Price			
Rent Price			
Rent-to-Price Ratio			
Wage Growth			
Unemployment Rate			

Questions to consider when determining your Market.

Does your local area support the deal types and deal tactics you're interested in? For example, if you're set on investing in short-term rentals, does your local area have good demand for STRs and an accommodating regulatory climate?

Can you afford to buy locally? Does the price point in your local market support your goals? Will you be able to scale faster locally or long-distance?

Does your local market offer the return profile you're looking for? Some markets are better for cash flow and others are better for appreciation.

Are the types of assets you want to buy available in your area? Are there mobile home parks for sale near you? What about small multifamily buildings? Different markets have different zoning laws and different housing supply. Check to make sure your desired market has the types of assets you want to invest in.

Are you interested in owner occupancy? This low-money-down operating plan option obviously requires local investing.

_____

_____

How well do you know the local market? There is an advantage to investing in a market you understand deeply. But if you're new to an area, the market knowledge advantage you get from investing locally is minimal.

_____

_____

Investing long-distance requires that you build a great team. Are you comfortable managing a team remotely?

_____

_____

Questions for the Long-Distance Market investor.

Which markets have an abundance of the deal types you are looking for?

_____

_____

_____

_____

Which markets have the profit potential you need right now?

_____

_____

_____

_____

_____

Are there certain areas of the country with a price point that is attractive to you?

_____

_____

Which markets have the best macroeconomic conditions that support (but don't guarantee!) future growth?

_____

_____

_____

_____

How are local housing market conditions in the markets you are considering?

_____

_____

_____

_____

_____

Home Prices

NOTES:

Rent Prices

NOTES:

Rent-to-Price Ratio

NOTES:

Economic Climate

NOTES:

Property Taxes

NOTES:

Regulatory Environment

NOTES:

Zoning

NOTES:

Schools

NOTES:

Crime Rate

NOTES:

Amenities and Proximity

NOTES:

X Factors

NOTES:

Use this rubric to determine which Markets are aligned with your resources, and your risk/reward preferences. Then, decide which Markets belong on your PREP.

	Resource Alignment			Risk/Reward Alignment	
	Time	Capital	Skill		Include in PREP?
Market 1:					
Market 2:					
Market 3:					
Market 4:					
Market 5:					

PROPERTY CLASSES

STRATEGIC DECISION: Select which property classes are aligned with your Vision and overall strategy. Write down all that apply on your PREP. For full instructions, see pages 293–294 in *Start with Strategy*.

Questions to consider when determining Property Classes.

What property classes work best with your intended deal types? Some property classes are better suited for specific deal types than others.

_____

_____

_____

_____

How do the operating plans you are considering align with various property classes? For example, if you want to do a BRRRR, buying Class A won't work. You'll need to invest in a property class with room for value-add.

_____

_____

_____

_____

_____

_____

Which class best represents your preferred Risk/Reward Profile?

_____

_____

_____

_____

Do you have the skills needed to manage major renovations and more difficult tenant management circumstances?

_____

_____

Do you want your investment to cash-flow from day one or are you willing to stabilize the asset yourself?

_____

_____

_____

Given your time preferences, which property class would be best for you?

_____

_____

_____

_____

Class A: Best-In-Class Properties

NOTES:

Class B: Average Properties

NOTES:

Class C: Below-Average Properties

NOTES:

Class D: Uninhabitable Properties

┌─ NOTES: ──┐
│   │
│   │
│   │
│   │
│   │
│   │
│   │
│   │
│   │
│   │
│   │
│   │
└──┘

Use this rubric to determine which Property Classes are aligned with your resources, and your risk/reward preferences. Then, decide which Property Classes belong on your PREP.

	Resource Alignment			Risk/Reward Alignment	
	Time	Capital	Skill		Include in PREP?
Class A					
Class B					
Class C					
Class D					

Use this space for any additional notes on your Deal Design.

DEAL DESIGN SUMMARY

Let's put it all together now. Complete the following based on your work in Part II.

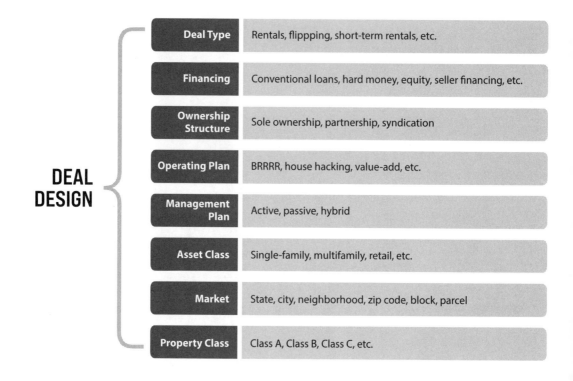

DEAL DESIGN

Deal Type	Rentals, flippping, short-term rentals, etc.
Financing	Conventional loans, hard money, equity, seller financing, etc.
Ownership Structure	Sole ownership, partnership, syndication
Operating Plan	BRRRR, house hacking, value-add, etc.
Management Plan	Active, passive, hybrid
Asset Class	Single-family, multifamily, retail, etc.
Market	State, city, neighborhood, zip code, block, parcel
Property Class	Class A, Class B, Class C, etc.

DEAL DESIGN

Deal Type

Ownership Structure

Financing

Operational Plan

Management Plan

Asset Class

Location

Property Class

PART IV
PORTFOLIO MANAGEMENT

VISION

DEAL DESIGN

PORTFOLIO MANAGEMENT

The last step in personalizing your portfolio is the most granular. This is called Portfolio Management, and it's where you make short-term decisions about how to grow your portfolio in the immediate future.

Portfolio Management is made up of several different exercises. First, it requires taking stock of your existing deals (if you have any) and seeing how they're performing. Then, you need to look externally and analyze what's happening in the economy, and the markets you operate in. With this research in hand, you can make decisions about how to allocate your resources, and how to scale more effectively. Once you have that all done, you will summarize your short-term plans into an Investment Thesis, Action Plan, and Buy Box.

Some of the exercises required for good Portfolio Management may be new to you. But that's okay—that's what the journal is for! Each chapter below has exercises, references, and questions to help you develop an action plan that will give you a great chance of progressing towards your goals. Some of the exercises are fully contained within the Journal—others (specifically the Portfolio Tracking chapter) will rely heavily on the Strategy Toolkit. It's just not easy to track your portfolio by hand. Trust me, you're better off using a computer.

Because Portfolio Management is about short-term thinking, I recommend you revisit this part of your strategy four times per year (once per quarter). This will allow you to properly manage risk, keep tabs on future opportunities, and optimize your performance. As such, the journal has four sets of each exercise, so you can continue to use it for the remainder of this yet. If you don't already monitor your portfolio regularly, I recommend you set a time in your calendar for three months from today to revisit your Portfolio Management plan. You don't want to forget!

When you're done with this part of the journal you'll have a completed PREP, and a fully personalized real estate plan. Make sure you write it down in the master PREP file on pages 12-13. Then, all you have to do is go out there and execute. Get to it!

PORTFOLIO TRACKING

STRATEGIC ACTIVITY: Track your current portfolio's composition and performance, if you have one. Write down the following key metrics in your PREP: total equity, total cash flow, average Return on Equity (ROE), average risk, and monthly time commitment. If you're new to investing and haven't yet participated in a deal, you can skip this section of your PREP. For full instructions, see pages 311–315 in *Start with Strategy*.

Now it's time to track your portfolio. You should complete a portfolio analysis four times a year. Use the Excel Toolkit located on www.BiggerPockets.com/strategybook to learn how to effectively track your portfolio. You can see examples of effective Portfolio Tracking on pages 306–311 in *Start with Strategy*.

Use this space to take notes on Portfolio Tracking.

NOTES:

Complete the following four times a year.

1 DATE EVALUATED: _____

Current Cashflow _____

Current Portfolio Value _____

Over-performing properties

_____

_____

_____

_____

Under-performing properties

_____

_____

_____

_____

DEAL DESIGN NOTES: _____

Portfolio risks

_____
_____
_____
_____
_____

┌─ *TIME ALLOCATION NOTES:* ──────────────────────
│
│
│
│
└───

┌─ *CAPITAL ALLOCATION NOTES:* ───────────────────
│
│
│
│
└───

┌─ *SKILL ALLOCATION NOTES:* ─────────────────────
│
│
│
│
└───

┌─ *POTENTIAL OPPORTUNITY NOTES:* ────────────────
│
│
│
└───

Progress to cashflow goal _____

Progress to PV Goal (%) _____

Considerations when reviewing your portfolio.

Are your deals offering similar financial performance?

_____

_____

How balanced is your portfolio in terms of deal tactics?

_____

_____

How much capital do you have invested?

_____

_____

Is your committed time aligned with your Vision?

_____

_____

Are you properly utilizing your skills?

_____

_____

What are the risk levels of each of your deals?

_____

_____

_____

_____

_____

2 DATE EVALUATED: _____

Current Cashflow _____

Current Portfolio Value _____

Over-performing properties

_____

_____

_____

_____

Under-performing properties

_____

_____

_____

_____

DEAL DESIGN NOTES:

Portfolio risks

_____
_____
_____
_____

TIME ALLOCATION NOTES:

CAPITAL ALLOCATION NOTES:

SKILL ALLOCATION NOTES:

POTENTIAL OPPORTUNITY NOTES:

Progress to cashflow goal _____

Progress to PV Goal (%) _____

Considerations when reviewing your portfolio.

Are your deals offering similar financial performance?

How balanced is your portfolio in terms of deal tactics?

How much capital do you have invested?

Is your committed time aligned with your Vision?

Are you properly utilizing your skills?

What are the risk levels of each of your deals?

(3) DATE EVALUATED: _____

Current Cashflow _____

Current Portfolio Value _____

Over-performing properties

_____

_____

_____

_____

Under-performing properties

_____

_____

_____

_____

DEAL DESIGN NOTES:

Portfolio risks

_____

_____

_____

_____

_____

TIME ALLOCATION NOTES:

CAPITAL ALLOCATION NOTES:

SKILL ALLOCATION NOTES:

POTENTIAL OPPORTUNITY NOTES:

Progress to cashflow goal _____

Progress to PV Goal (%) _____

Considerations when reviewing your portfolio.

Are your deals offering similar financial performance?

_____

_____

How balanced is your portfolio in terms of deal tactics?

_____

_____

How much capital do you have invested?

_____

_____

Is your committed time aligned with your Vision?

_____

_____

Are you properly utilizing your skills?

_____

_____

What are the risk levels of each of your deals?

_____

_____

_____

_____

4 DATE EVALUATED: _____

Current Cashflow _____

Current Portfolio Value _____

Over-performing properties

_____
_____
_____
_____

Under-performing properties

_____
_____
_____
_____

DEAL DESIGN NOTES: _____

Portfolio risks

_____

_____

_____

_____

TIME ALLOCATION NOTES:

CAPITAL ALLOCATION NOTES:

SKILL ALLOCATION NOTES:

POTENTIAL OPPORTUNITY NOTES:

Progress to cashflow goal _____

Progress to PV Goal (%) _____

Considerations when reviewing your portfolio.

Are your deals offering similar financial performance?

_____

_____

How balanced is your portfolio in terms of deal tactics?

_____

_____

How much capital do you have invested?

_____

_____

Is your committed time aligned with your Vision?

_____

_____

Are you properly utilizing your skills?

_____

_____

What are the risk levels of each of your deals?

_____

_____

_____

_____

_____

BUSINESS CYCLE

STRATEGIC ACTIVITY: Determine what stage of the business cycle we're in currently, to the best of your ability. Once you've made your assessment, write it down in your PREP, and take time to consider if your current tactics are appropriate given the macroeconomic environment. For full instructions, see pages 323–324 in *Start with Strategy*.

The periodic cycles that an economy goes through are known as the "business cycle." The business cycle has four distinct phases: expansions, peaks, recessions, and troughs. Every business cycle is unique; no two recessions are identical, and neither are any two expansions. Although there is variance between cycles, it is still very helpful to understand the general patterns of the business cycle, as they are roughly correlated with different real estate investing tactics.

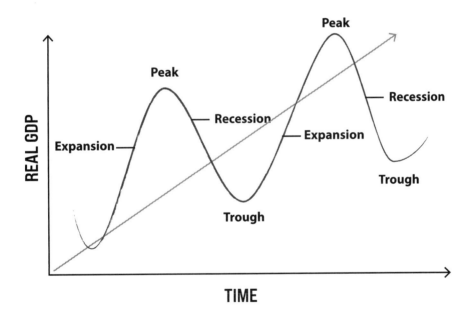

1 DATE EVALUATED: _____

Business Cycle Assessment:

GROSS DOMESTIC PRODUCT (GDP): _____   **INTEREST RATES:** _____

UNEMPLOYMENT: _____   **INFLATION:** _____

NOTES:

Current Business Cycle Phase:

_____

_____

_____

Questions to consider when evaluating your economic environment.

What phase of the business cycle do you think we're in? How confident do you feel in your assessment?

_____

_____

_____

Are you currently using tactics that are appropriate given the phase of the business cycle we're in?

_____

_____

_____

_____

_____

What is the best way to deploy your resources given the macroeconomic climate?

_____

_____

_____

_____

_____

_____

_____

What is your personal assessment of the current market risk?

_____

_____

_____

_____

_____

_____

_____

_____

How have the risk levels of your existing portfolio and your planned tactics changed? Have the prices of risk-free assets like bonds and money market accounts changed since your last assessment? If so, are your risk premiums still appropriate?

_____

_____

_____

_____

_____

_____

_____

_____

What impact is the business cycle having on the non–real estate elements of your portfolio? Is your job or transactional income at risk due to a potential recession? What about your family—could any of them lose their job? Conversely, are times improving and can you expect a raise?

_____

_____

_____

_____

_____

_____

_____

_____

_____

_____

_____

(2) DATE EVALUATED: _____

Business Cycle Assessment:

GROSS DOMESTIC PRODUCT (GDP): _____   **INTEREST RATES:** _____

UNEMPLOYMENT: _____   **INFLATION:** _____

NOTES:

Current Business Cycle Phase:

_____

_____

_____

Questions to consider when evaluating your economic environment.

What phase of the business cycle do you think we're in? How confident do you feel in your assessment?

_____

_____

_____

Are you currently using tactics that are appropriate given the phase of the business cycle we're in?

What is the best way to deploy your resources given the macroeconomic climate?

What is your personal assessment of the current market risk?

How have the risk levels of your existing portfolio and your planned tactics changed? Have the prices of risk-free assets like bonds and money market accounts changed since your last assessment? If so, are your risk premiums still appropriate?

_____

_____

_____

_____

_____

_____

_____

_____

What impact is the business cycle having on the non–real estate elements of your portfolio? Is your job or transactional income at risk due to a potential recession? What about your family—could any of them lose their job? Conversely, are times improving and can you expect a raise?

_____

_____

_____

_____

_____

_____

_____

_____

_____

_____

(3) DATE EVALUATED: _____

Business Cycle Assessment:

GROSS DOMESTIC PRODUCT (GDP): _____ **INTEREST RATES:** _____

UNEMPLOYMENT: _____ **INFLATION:** _____

NOTES:

Current Business Cycle Phase:

_____

_____

_____

Questions to consider when evaluating your economic environment.

What phase of the business cycle do you think we're in? How confident do you feel in your assessment?

_____

_____

_____

Are you currently using tactics that are appropriate given the phase of the business cycle we're in?

_____

_____

_____

_____

_____

What is the best way to deploy your resources given the macroeconomic climate?

_____

_____

_____

_____

_____

_____

_____

_____

What is your personal assessment of the current market risk?

_____

_____

_____

_____

_____

_____

_____

_____

_____

_____

How have the risk levels of your existing portfolio and your planned tactics changed? Have the prices of risk-free assets like bonds and money market accounts changed since your last assessment? If so, are your risk premiums still appropriate?

_____

_____

_____

_____

_____

_____

_____

_____

What impact is the business cycle having on the non–real estate elements of your portfolio? Is your job or transactional income at risk due to a potential recession? What about your family—could any of them lose their job? Conversely, are times improving and can you expect a raise?

_____

_____

_____

_____

_____

_____

_____

_____

_____

_____

_____

4 DATE EVALUATED: _____

Business Cycle Assessment:

GROSS DOMESTIC PRODUCT (GDP): _____ **INTEREST RATES:** _____

UNEMPLOYMENT: _____ **INFLATION:** _____

NOTES:

Current Business Cycle Phase:

_____

_____

_____

Questions to consider when evaluating your economic environment.

What phase of the business cycle do you think we're in? How confident do you feel in your assessment?

_____

_____

_____

Are you currently using tactics that are appropriate given the phase of the business cycle we're in?

_____

_____

_____

_____

What is the best way to deploy your resources given the macroeconomic climate?

_____

_____

_____

_____

_____

_____

What is your personal assessment of the current market risk?

_____

_____

_____

_____

_____

_____

_____

_____

How have the risk levels of your existing portfolio and your planned tactics changed? Have the prices of risk-free assets like bonds and money market accounts changed since your last assessment? If so, are your risk premiums still appropriate?

_____

_____

_____

_____

_____

_____

_____

_____

What impact is the business cycle having on the non–real estate elements of your portfolio? Is your job or transactional income at risk due to a potential recession? What about your family—could any of them lose their job? Conversely, are times improving and can you expect a raise?

_____

_____

_____

_____

_____

_____

_____

_____

_____

_____

_____

LOCAL MARKET CONDITIONS

STRATEGIC ACTIVITY: Research local market conditions and develop benchmarks. Focus on getting a sense of how the economy and housing market are trending in any market you currently invest in, or are considering investing in. Then, analyze deals and talk to local investors to learn what deals are currently available in your markets, and establish benchmarks. Once you're done, write down your benchmarks and any key insights on your PREP. For full instructions, see pages 330–331 in *Start with Strategy*.

You should research your Local Market Conditions four times per year. List out your Deal Designs, and evaluate their Return on Equity and Annual Equity Growth (estimations are okay!). Based on this evaluation, determine the Market Condition. You can find examples of determining Market Conditions and Market Benchmarks on pages 326–330 in *Start with Strategy*.

Use this space to take notes on Local Market Conditions.

NOTES:

1 DATE EVALUATED: _____

Market 1 Benchmarks

Market: _____

DEAL DESIGN	RETURN ON EQUITY (EST)	ANNUAL EQUITY GROWTH (EST)
1:		
2:		
3:		

Market Condition: (Circle one)   **Buyer's Market   Seller's Market   Balanced Market**

Market 2 Benchmarks

Market: _____

DEAL DESIGN	RETURN ON EQUITY (EST)	ANNUAL EQUITY GROWTH (EST)
1:		
2:		
3:		

Market Condition: (Circle one)   **Buyer's Market   Seller's Market   Balanced Market**

Market 3 Benchmarks

Market: _____

DEAL DESIGN	RETURN ON EQUITY (EST)	ANNUAL EQUITY GROWTH (EST)
1:		
2:		
3:		

Market Condition: (Circle one)   **Buyer's Market   Seller's Market   Balanced Market**

Questions to consider when determining your Local Market Conditions.

What do the economic conditions in your areas mean to you and your portfolio? How are unemployment, wage growth, and population trending?

_____

_____

_____

_____

Are the conditions in your target markets attractive for new investments? Are the price points and rental incomes desirable, or would an alternative market be better?

_____

_____

_____

Who has the leverage in your markets? If sellers have an advantage, should you consider selling? As a buyer, how should you adjust your Deal Design to account for your current negotiating leverage?

_____

_____

_____

_____

_____

Of all your Deal Design options, which do you think will work best in current conditions?

_____

_____

_____

_____

_____

② DATE EVALUATED: _____

Market 1 Benchmarks

Market: _____

DEAL DESIGN	RETURN ON EQUITY (EST)	ANNUAL EQUITY GROWTH (EST)
1:		
2:		
3:		

Market Condition: (Circle one)   **Buyer's Market**   **Seller's Market**   **Balanced Market**

Market 2 Benchmarks

Market: _____

DEAL DESIGN	RETURN ON EQUITY (EST)	ANNUAL EQUITY GROWTH (EST)
1:		
2:		
3:		

Market Condition: (Circle one)   **Buyer's Market**   **Seller's Market**   **Balanced Market**

Market 3 Benchmarks

Market: _____

DEAL DESIGN	RETURN ON EQUITY (EST)	ANNUAL EQUITY GROWTH (EST)
1:		
2:		
3:		

Market Condition: (Circle one)   **Buyer's Market**   **Seller's Market**   **Balanced Market**

Questions to consider when determining your Local Market Conditions.

What do the economic conditions in your areas mean to you and your portfolio? How are unemployment, wage growth, and population trending?

Are the conditions in your target markets attractive for new investments? Are the price points and rental incomes desirable, or would an alternative market be better?

Who has the leverage in your markets? If sellers have an advantage, should you consider selling? As a buyer, how should you adjust your Deal Design to account for your current negotiating leverage?

Of all your Deal Design options, which do you think will work best in current conditions?

3 DATE EVALUATED: _____

Market 1 Benchmarks

Market: _____

DEAL DESIGN	RETURN ON EQUITY (EST)	ANNUAL EQUITY GROWTH (EST)
1:		
2:		
3:		

Market Condition: (Circle one)   **Buyer's Market**   **Seller's Market**   **Balanced Market**

Market 2 Benchmarks

Market: _____

DEAL DESIGN	RETURN ON EQUITY (EST)	ANNUAL EQUITY GROWTH (EST)
1:		
2:		
3:		

Market Condition: (Circle one)   **Buyer's Market**   **Seller's Market**   **Balanced Market**

Market 3 Benchmarks

Market: _____

DEAL DESIGN	RETURN ON EQUITY (EST)	ANNUAL EQUITY GROWTH (EST)
1:		
2:		
3:		

Market Condition: (Circle one)   **Buyer's Market**   **Seller's Market**   **Balanced Market**

Questions to consider when determining your Local Market Conditions.

What do the economic conditions in your areas mean to you and your portfolio? How are unemployment, wage growth, and population trending?

_____

_____

_____

_____

Are the conditions in your target markets attractive for new investments? Are the price points and rental incomes desirable, or would an alternative market be better?

_____

_____

_____

Who has the leverage in your markets? If sellers have an advantage, should you consider selling? As a buyer, how should you adjust your Deal Design to account for your current negotiating leverage?

_____

_____

_____

_____

Of all your Deal Design options, which do you think will work best in current conditions?

_____

_____

_____

_____

4 DATE EVALUATED: _____

Market 1 Benchmarks

Market: _____

DEAL DESIGN	RETURN ON EQUITY (EST)	ANNUAL EQUITY GROWTH (EST)
1:		
2:		
3:		

Market Condition: *(Circle one)*   **Buyer's Market**   **Seller's Market**   **Balanced Market**

Market 2 Benchmarks

Market: _____

DEAL DESIGN	RETURN ON EQUITY (EST)	ANNUAL EQUITY GROWTH (EST)
1:		
2:		
3:		

Market Condition: *(Circle one)*   **Buyer's Market**   **Seller's Market**   **Balanced Market**

Market 3 Benchmarks

Market: _____

DEAL DESIGN	RETURN ON EQUITY (EST)	ANNUAL EQUITY GROWTH (EST)
1:		
2:		
3:		

Market Condition: *(Circle one)*   **Buyer's Market**   **Seller's Market**   **Balanced Market**

Questions to consider when determining your Local Market Conditions.

What do the economic conditions in your areas mean to you and your portfolio? How are unemployment, wage growth, and population trending?

_____

_____

_____

_____

Are the conditions in your target markets attractive for new investments? Are the price points and rental incomes desirable, or would an alternative market be better?

_____

_____

_____

Who has the leverage in your markets? If sellers have an advantage, should you consider selling? As a buyer, how should you adjust your Deal Design to account for your current negotiating leverage?

_____

_____

_____

_____

_____

Of all your Deal Design options, which do you think will work best in current conditions?

_____

_____

_____

_____

_____

RESOURCE ALLOCATION

Now it's time to track your Resource Allocation. You should complete an audit of your Resource Allocation four times a year. Use the Excel Toolkit located on www.BiggerPockets.com/strategybook to learn how to effectively determine your Resource Allocation.

Use this space to take notes on Resource Allocation.

_____

_____

_____

_____

_____

_____

_____

_____

Below is a sample on how to effectively track your Resource Allocation. Again, you should be tracking this items four times a year.

CURRENT RESOURCE INPUTS	DEAL 1	DEAL 2	DEAL 3
Estimated Equity Value	$85,115	$92,798	$79,290
Monthly Time Invested (Hours)	5	9	3
Skills	Tenant management, repairs, operations	Tenant management, repairs, operations	Portfolio Management, Partner Management

1 DATE EVALUATED: _____

CURRENT RESOURCE INPUTS	DEAL 1	DEAL 2	DEAL 3
Estimated Equity Value			
Monthly Time Invested (Hours)			
Skills			

ALTERNATIVE OPTIONS NOTES:

REALLOCATION RESOURCE INPUTS	DEAL 1	DEAL 2	DEAL 3
Estimated Equity Value			
Monthly Time Invested (Hours)			
Skills			

Questions to consider as you evaluate your Resource Allocation.

Are your current resources generating the types of returns you're looking for? Are your returns coming from the best profit drivers?

Do any of your deals require an outsized number of resources? Are any of your deals particularly efficient at using resources?

How diversified is your Resource Allocation? Are all of your resources invested into similar Deal Designs or are you diversified?

How many resources do you have to pursue additional deals? Do you have the capital, time, and skill to take on a new investment? Or do you need to reallocate away from a current deal to pursue the next one?

Would adding new resources to current deals improve performance or diversification? Or are new resources best used on a new deal?

_____

_____

_____

_____

If you are going to reallocate resources, is the benefit of reallocation greater than the cost and hassle of reallocation?

_____

_____

_____

_____

When reallocating capital, will you pursue a refinance or a sale?

_____

_____

NOTES:

(2) DATE EVALUATED: _____

CURRENT RESOURCE INPUTS	DEAL 1	DEAL 2	DEAL 3
Estimated Equity Value			
Monthly Time Invested (Hours)			
Skills			

ALTERNATIVE OPTIONS NOTES:

REALLOCATION RESOURCE INPUTS	DEAL 1	DEAL 2	DEAL 3
Estimated Equity Value			
Monthly Time Invested (Hours)			
Skills			

Questions to consider as you evaluate your Resource Allocation.

Are your current resources generating the types of returns you're looking for? Are your returns coming from the best profit drivers?

Do any of your deals require an outsized number of resources? Are any of your deals particularly efficient at using resources?

How diversified is your Resource Allocation? Are all of your resources invested into similar Deal Designs or are you diversified?

How many resources do you have to pursue additional deals? Do you have the capital, time, and skill to take on a new investment? Or do you need to reallocate away from a current deal to pursue the next one?

Would adding new resources to current deals improve performance or diversification? Or are new resources best used on a new deal?

_____

_____

_____

_____

If you are going to reallocate resources, is the benefit of reallocation greater than the cost and hassle of reallocation?

_____

_____

_____

_____

When reallocating capital, will you pursue a refinance or a sale?

_____

_____

_____

NOTES:

3 DATE EVALUATED: _____

CURRENT RESOURCE INPUTS	DEAL 1	DEAL 2	DEAL 3
Estimated Equity Value			
Monthly Time Invested (Hours)			
Skills			

ALTERNATIVE OPTIONS NOTES: _____

REALLOCATION RESOURCE INPUTS	DEAL 1	DEAL 2	DEAL 3
Estimated Equity Value			
Monthly Time Invested (Hours)			
Skills			

Questions to consider as you evaluate your Resource Allocation.

Are your current resources generating the types of returns you're looking for? Are your returns coming from the best profit drivers?

Do any of your deals require an outsized number of resources? Are any of your deals particularly efficient at using resources?

How diversified is your Resource Allocation? Are all of your resources invested into similar Deal Designs or are you diversified?

How many resources do you have to pursue additional deals? Do you have the capital, time, and skill to take on a new investment? Or do you need to reallocate away from a current deal to pursue the next one?

Would adding new resources to current deals improve performance or diversification? Or are new resources best used on a new deal?

_____

_____

_____

_____

If you are going to reallocate resources, is the benefit of reallocation greater than the cost and hassle of reallocation?

_____

_____

_____

_____

When reallocating capital, will you pursue a refinance or a sale?

_____

_____

NOTES:

(4) DATE EVALUATED: _____

CURRENT RESOURCE INPUTS	DEAL 1	DEAL 2	DEAL 3
Estimated Equity Value			
Monthly Time Invested (Hours)			
Skills			

ALTERNATIVE OPTIONS NOTES:

REALLOCATION RESOURCE INPUTS	DEAL 1	DEAL 2	DEAL 3
Estimated Equity Value			
Monthly Time Invested (Hours)			
Skills			

Questions to consider as you evaluate your Resource Allocation.

Are your current resources generating the types of returns you're looking for? Are your returns coming from the best profit drivers?

Do any of your deals require an outsized number of resources? Are any of your deals particularly efficient at using resources?

How diversified is your Resource Allocation? Are all of your resources invested into similar Deal Designs or are you diversified?

How many resources do you have to pursue additional deals? Do you have the capital, time, and skill to take on a new investment? Or do you need to reallocate away from a current deal to pursue the next one?

Would adding new resources to current deals improve performance or diversification? Or are new resources best used on a new deal?

_____

_____

_____

_____

If you are going to reallocate resources, is the benefit of reallocation greater than the cost and hassle of reallocation?

_____

_____

_____

_____

When reallocating capital, will you pursue a refinance or a sale?

_____

_____

NOTES:

SCALING PATHS

Questions to consider when Scaling Paths.

What scaling path best aligns with your skill set? What path aligns with your time resource?

How big are your goals? If you want to get big quickly, you'll need to pursue more aggressive (and higher-risk) scaling plans. Those who want to grow steadily can pursue less risky options.

What operations do you want to take on? Are you interested in managing a full-time in-house team? Or would you prefer to work with third-party contractors?

Do you want to specialize in one market or are you willing to build out a team and operations across multiple markets?

How close are you to your time horizon? If you're far from your time horizon, you can pursue equity growth and higher-risk investments. If you're close to your horizon, you may want to consider de-risking, deleveraging, and moving toward cash flow.

Scaling Quantity

NOTES:

Scaling Size

NOTES:

Liquidity Balanced Scaling

NOTES:

Dollar Cost Averaging

NOTES:

Equity to Cashflow

NOTES:

Active to Passive

NOTES:

In-House Scaling

NOTES:

Maintenance Mode

NOTES:

Other

NOTES:

INTENDED SCALING PATHS

ACTION PLAN

STRATEGIC ACTIVITY: Write out an Investment Thesis, develop your Tactical Plan, and craft your Buy Box. Ensure these three elements of your Action Plan are aligned with one another, and when they are, write them in your PREP. Take time to make sure that all of your actions are aligned with your Vision and your Deal Design before finalizing your strategy. For full instructions, see pages 367–370 in *Start with Strategy*.

Here is an example of the PREP work.

Investment Thesis

- Continue working W-2 job while focusing portfolio on tax-advantaged equity growth. Cash flow is required for all deals but is not a priority.
- Despite slightly under-risked portfolio, continue to favor more conservative investments due to uncertain economic conditions.
- Trade out any current deals that aren't meeting benchmarks.
- Although the macroeconomic environment is cloudy, local market conditions are stable. Focus on scaling vertically in Charlotte, North Carolina, and becoming an expert in current location.
- Use only hybrid management plans to maintain twenty-hour time commitment per month while allowing for future scale.
- Look for opportunities for commercial real estate deal within twelve to twenty-four months.

Action Plan

- Deploy $100,000 in capital into syndication or funds.
- Complete cosmetic upgrades to Deal 2, and list for sale within 3 months.
- Purchase value-add rental property using 1031 exchange from Deal 2 proceeds within ninety days of Deal 2 sale.
- Set aside $20,000 current investable assets for wedding.
- Network with at least ten commercial real estate investors in the next year, and identify potential partners.
- Read The Multifamily Millionaire Volumes 1 & 2 within six months.
- Grow investable assets to $100,000 for use in first commercial property within eighteen months.
- Develop Buy Box for commercial purchase once networking and education goals are complete.

Buy Box

- **Deal Type:** Rental property
- **Management Plan:** Hybrid
- **Business Plan:** Buy and hold
- **Financing:** Conventional, portfolio loans
- **Asset Class:** 1–4 units residential
- **Ownership Structure:** Sole ownership/partnership
- **Property Class:** B
- **Location:** Charlotte, North Carolina
- **Purchase Price:** $250,000–$450,000
- **Rehab Costs:** < $5,000
- **Risk Target:** 2 or 3
- **ROE Target:** 7%+

1 DATE EVALUATED: _____

Questions to consider when writing your Investment Thesis.

Of all the Deal Designs you selected in Part 3, which will best support your Vision in the coming years, given current market conditions?

_____

_____

_____

What is your Transactional Income Plan? Would a career change better support your Vision or lifestyle?

_____

_____

_____

Can you—and do you—want to invest in any new deals in the coming months or years? If so, will you follow a scaling plan? How will you procure the necessary resources to achieve your next deal?

_____

_____

_____

_____

Is your current resource allocation optimal or can your resources be put to better use?

_____

_____

_____

What liquidity will you need from your portfolio in the coming months? Are there any major life events or expenses outside of real estate you need to plan for?

_____

_____

_____

_____

What new skills do you want to learn?

_____

_____

_____

_____

Is there anything you want to accomplish a year or two from now that you can start working toward today?

_____

_____

_____

Investment Thesis

_____

_____

_____

_____

_____

_____

_____

Questions to consider when determining your Tactical Plan.

Do I plan to buy any deals in the near future?

_____

What Deal Designs are going to work best for me right now?

_____

_____

_____

_____

Will I change any elements of my existing deals, like a new management or operational plan?

_____

_____

How can I execute on my reallocation plans?

_____

_____

_____

_____

Will I add any new resources to my portfolio?

_____

_____

Should I deploy my resources now or plan ahead a few months?

_____

_____

What tactics do I aspire to in the future, and what actions can I take today to help me get there?

_____

_____

_____

Are there any networking initiatives that would support my Vision?

_____

_____

Tactical Plan

_____

_____

_____

_____

_____

_____

_____

Questions to consider when building your Buy Box.

Which Deal Design options support your beliefs about the current phase of the business cycle?

_____

_____

_____

What types of deals can you execute on today, given your resources? What can you afford?

_____

_____

_____

What Deal Designs do you have the skills to operate well?

_____

_____

_____

Which Deal Designs are aligned with your current risk capacity and tolerance?

_____

_____

_____

Which deals would support your desired profit drivers and return targets?

_____

_____

_____

Complete:

Buy Box

- **Deal Type:** _____
- **Property Class:** _____

- **Management Plan:** _____
- **Location:** _____

- **Business Plan:** _____
- **Purchase Price:** _____

- **Financing:** _____
- **Rehab Costs:** _____

- **Asset Class:** _____
- **Risk Target:** _____

- **Ownership Structure:** _____
- **ROE Target:** _____

② DATE EVALUATED: _____

Questions to consider when writing your Investment Thesis.

Of all the Deal Designs you selected in Part 3, which will best support your Vision in the coming years, given current market conditions?

_____

_____

_____

What is your Transactional Income Plan? Would a career change better support your Vision or lifestyle?

_____

_____

_____

Can you—and do you—want to invest in any new deals in the coming months or years? If so, will you follow a scaling plan? How will you procure the necessary resources to achieve your next deal?

_____

_____

_____

_____

Is your current resource allocation optimal or can your resources be put to better use?

_____

_____

_____

_____

What liquidity will you need from your portfolio in the coming months? Are there any major life events or expenses outside of real estate you need to plan for?

_____

_____

_____

_____

What new skills do you want to learn?

_____

_____

_____

_____

Is there anything you want to accomplish a year or two from now that you can start working toward today?

_____

_____

_____

Investment Thesis

_____

_____

_____

_____

_____

_____

_____

Questions to consider when determining your Tactical Plan.

Do I plan to buy any deals in the near future?

What Deal Designs are going to work best for me right now?

Will I change any elements of my existing deals, like a new management or operational plan?

How can I execute on my reallocation plans?

Will I add any new resources to my portfolio?

Should I deploy my resources now or plan ahead a few months?

What tactics do I aspire to in the future, and what actions can I take today to help me get there?

_____

_____

_____

Are there any networking initiatives that would support my Vision?

_____

_____

Tactical Plan

_____

_____

_____

_____

_____

_____

_____

Questions to consider when building your Buy Box.

Which Deal Design options support your beliefs about the current phase of the business cycle?

_____

_____

_____

What types of deals can you execute on today, given your resources? What can you afford?

_____

_____

_____

What Deal Designs do you have the skills to operate well?

_____

_____

_____

Which Deal Designs are aligned with your current risk capacity and tolerance?

_____

_____

_____

Which deals would support your desired profit drivers and return targets?

_____

_____

_____

Complete:

Buy Box

- **Deal Type:** _____
- **Management Plan:** _____
- **Business Plan:** _____
- **Financing:** _____
- **Asset Class:** _____
- **Ownership Structure:** _____

- **Property Class:** _____
- **Location:** _____
- **Purchase Price:** _____
- **Rehab Costs:** _____
- **Risk Target:** _____
- **ROE Target:** _____

(3) DATE EVALUATED: _____

Questions to consider when writing your Investment Thesis.

Of all the Deal Designs you selected in Part 3, which will best support your Vision in the coming years, given current market conditions?

_____
_____
_____

What is your Transactional Income Plan? Would a career change better support your Vision or lifestyle?

_____
_____
_____
_____

Can you—and do you—want to invest in any new deals in the coming months or years? If so, will you follow a scaling plan? How will you procure the necessary resources to achieve your next deal?

_____
_____
_____
_____
_____

Is your current resource allocation optimal or can your resources be put to better use?

_____
_____
_____
_____

What liquidity will you need from your portfolio in the coming months? Are there any major life events or expenses outside of real estate you need to plan for?

_____

_____

_____

_____

What new skills do you want to learn?

_____

_____

_____

_____

Is there anything you want to accomplish a year or two from now that you can start working toward today?

_____

_____

_____

Investment Thesis

_____

_____

_____

_____

_____

_____

_____

Questions to consider when determining your Tactical Plan.

Do I plan to buy any deals in the near future?

_____

What Deal Designs are going to work best for me right now?

_____

_____

_____

_____

Will I change any elements of my existing deals, like a new management or operational plan?

_____

_____

How can I execute on my reallocation plans?

_____

_____

_____

_____

Will I add any new resources to my portfolio?

_____

_____

Should I deploy my resources now or plan ahead a few months?

_____

_____

What tactics do I aspire to in the future, and what actions can I take today to help me get there?

Are there any networking initiatives that would support my Vision?

Tactical Plan

Questions to consider when building your Buy Box.

Which Deal Design options support your beliefs about the current phase of the business cycle?

What types of deals can you execute on today, given your resources? What can you afford?

What Deal Designs do you have the skills to operate well?

_____

_____

_____

Which Deal Designs are aligned with your current risk capacity and tolerance?

_____

_____

_____

Which deals would support your desired profit drivers and return targets?

_____

_____

_____

Complete:

Buy Box

- **Deal Type:** _____
- **Property Class:** _____

- **Management Plan:** _____
- **Location:** _____

- **Business Plan:** _____
- **Purchase Price:** _____

- **Financing:** _____
- **Rehab Costs:** _____

- **Asset Class:** _____
- **Risk Target:** _____

- **Ownership Structure:** _____
- **ROE Target:** _____

④ DATE EVALUATED: _____

Questions to consider when writing your Investment Thesis.

Of all the Deal Designs you selected in Part 3, which will best support your Vision in the coming years, given current market conditions?

_____

_____

_____

What is your Transactional Income Plan? Would a career change better support your Vision or lifestyle?

_____

_____

_____

Can you—and do you—want to invest in any new deals in the coming months or years? If so, will you follow a scaling plan? How will you procure the necessary resources to achieve your next deal?

_____

_____

_____

_____

Is your current resource allocation optimal or can your resources be put to better use?

_____

_____

_____

_____

What liquidity will you need from your portfolio in the coming months? Are there any major life events or expenses outside of real estate you need to plan for?

_____

_____

_____

_____

What new skills do you want to learn?

_____

_____

_____

_____

Is there anything you want to accomplish a year or two from now that you can start working toward today?

_____

_____

_____

Investment Thesis

_____

_____

_____

_____

_____

_____

_____

_____

Questions to consider when determining your Tactical Plan.

Do I plan to buy any deals in the near future?

What Deal Designs are going to work best for me right now?

Will I change any elements of my existing deals, like a new management or operational plan?

How can I execute on my reallocation plans?

Will I add any new resources to my portfolio?

Should I deploy my resources now or plan ahead a few months?

What tactics do I aspire to in the future, and what actions can I take today to help me get there?

_____

_____

_____

Are there any networking initiatives that would support my Vision?

_____

_____

Tactical Plan

_____

_____

_____

_____

_____

_____

_____

Questions to consider when building your Buy Box.

Which Deal Design options support your beliefs about the current phase of the business cycle?

_____

_____

_____

What types of deals can you execute on today, given your resources? What can you afford?

_____

_____

_____

What Deal Designs do you have the skills to operate well?

_____

_____

_____

Which Deal Designs are aligned with your current risk capacity and tolerance?

_____

_____

_____

Which deals would support your desired profit drivers and return targets?

_____

_____

_____

Complete:

Buy Box

- **Deal Type:** _____
- **Property Class:** _____

- **Management Plan:** _____
- **Location:** _____

- **Business Plan:** _____
- **Purchase Price:** _____

- **Financing:** _____
- **Rehab Costs:** _____

- **Asset Class:** _____
- **Risk Target:** _____

- **Ownership Structure:** _____
- **ROE Target:** _____

PORTFOLIO MANAGEMENT SUMMARY

Let's put it all together now. Complete the following based on your work in Part III.

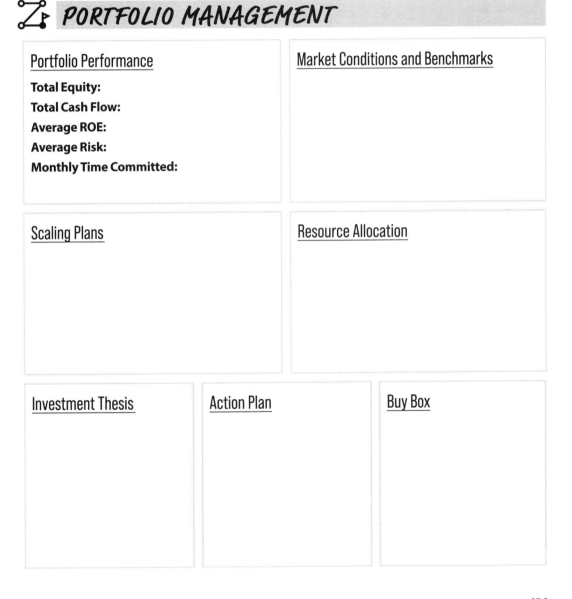

PORTFOLIO MANAGEMENT

Portfolio Performance

Total Equity:
Total Cash Flow:
Average ROE:
Average Risk:
Monthly Time Committed:

Market Conditions and Benchmarks

Scaling Plans

Resource Allocation

Investment Thesis

Action Plan

Buy Box

WRAPPING UP

You've done it! You've completed your PREP work and have a clear sense of your portfolio, present and future. You're now in an excellent place to pursue your financial goals through real estate investing. You understand the financial concepts and trade-offs that underpin portfolio growth. You have a Vision of the future you want to pursue. You know what Deal Designs can help you achieve your goals. And you have Portfolio Management skills to consistently move you forward. Combined, you have a personalized strategy that is designed to hit your specific goals. This in itself is an enormous accomplishment, and you should be proud of yourself. Many people aspire to take their financial future into their own hands, but few put in the work to do it in a systematic and sustainable way. You have, and that's a vital step on your financial journey.

Although you have completed this workbook, your strategy and your PREP will never truly be "done." As your goals, life circumstances, and personal preferences change, so will your strategy. As you reconsider your strategy and evolve as an investor, I encourage you to revisit this workbook frequently. The format of this book was chosen deliberately to help you complete your PREP for the first time, but also to serve as a reference guide when you inevitably update your strategy. This doesn't mean that you should be redoing your PREP over and over again in short intervals. That isn't helpful. The learning comes from crafting your plan, executing it, and learning from the results. Sometimes you're going to nail it. Some deals and Portfolio Management decisions are going to work out great. Other times, things won't go as planned. This is part of the process. Just try to keep getting better.

You have a Personal Real Estate Portfolio in front of you! It's time to put your plan in motion. Start working toward the Vision of the future you want to create!

BLANK PREP

 **VISION**

Personal Values

Resource Audit
Money:
Time:
Current Skills:

Risk Profile
Time Horizon:
Risk Tolerance:
Risk Capacity:
Current Risk Profile:

Transactional Income Plan

Financial Goals
Reinvestment Rate:

Residual Income Goal:

Portfolio Value Goal:

 DEAL DESIGN

Deal Type

Ownership Structure

Financing

Operational Plan

Management Plan

Asset Class

Location

Property Class

PORTFOLIO MANAGEMENT

Portfolio Performance

Total Equity:

Total Cash Flow:

Average ROE:

Average Risk:

Monthly Time Committed:

Market Conditions and Benchmarks

Scaling Plans

Resource Allocation

Investment Thesis

Action Plan

Buy Box

The BiggerPockets
CHECKLIST

- [ ] **Sign up for your free membership**
(biggerpockets.com/signup)

- [ ] **Introduce yourself and
your real estate goals in our forums**
(biggerpockets.com/forums)

- [ ] **Read a few blogs from
our expert writers**
(biggerpockets.com/blog)

- [ ] **Sign up for a free webinar with
our podcast hosts**
(biggerpockets.com/webinars)

- [ ] **Start networking with agents in
your market**
(biggerpockets.com/agentfinder)

- [ ] **Buy a book to learn more about
your real estate strategy**
(biggerpockets.com/store)

SUPERCHARGE YOUR REAL ESTATE INVESTING.

Get **exclusive bonus content** like checklists, contracts, interviews, and more when you buy from the BiggerPockets Bookstore.

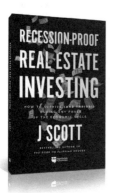
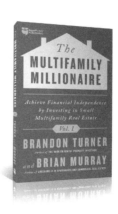

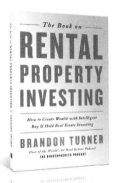

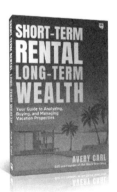

Looking for more?
Join the BiggerPockets Community

BiggerPockets brings together education, tools, and a community of more than 2+ million like-minded members—all in one place. Learn about investment strategies, analyze properties, connect with investor-friendly agents, and more.

Go to **biggerpockets.com** to learn more!

 Listen to a **BiggerPockets Podcast**

 Watch **BiggerPockets on YouTube**

 Join the **Community Forum**

 Learn more on **the Blog**

 Read more **BiggerPockets Books**

 Learn about our **Real Estate Investing Bootcamps**

 Connect with an **Investor-Friendly Real Estate Agent**

 Go Pro! Start, scale, and manage your portfolio with your **Pro Membership**

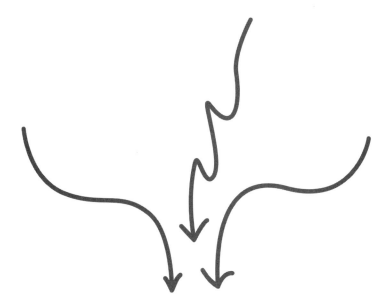

Follow us on social media!

Sign up for a Pro account and take **20 PERCENT OFF** with code **BOOKS20**.